*You*
**KNOW**
you're GAY
*when...*

# You
# **KNOW**
# you're GAY
# *when...*

## THOSE UNFORGETTABLE MOMENTS
## THAT MAKE US WHO WE ARE

*Joseph Cohen*

*Produced by Fresh Ideas Daily*

**CB**

**CONTEMPORARY BOOKS**

A TRIBUNE COMPANY

**Library of Congress Cataloging-in-Publication Data**

Cohen, Joseph, 1949–
    You know you're gay when … : those unforgettable moments
that make us who we are / Joseph Cohen.
       p.    cm.
    ISBN 0-8092-3320-7 (alk. paper)
    1. Gay men—Humor.    I. Title.
PN6231.H57C64    1995
818'.5402—dc20                               95-515
                                                  CIP

*Cover and interior design by* Tom Dolle
*Cover illustration by* Mary Sexton; *Photo credits* Bettmann: pp. 19, 36,
52, 58–59, 67, 85, 86, 102; Gregg Chicorelli: p. 44; Christopher &
Castro: p. 101; John DiGennaro: pp. 17, 29, 50–51, 90; Index Stock
Photography: opposite p. 1, pp. 24, 34–35, 42, 49, 77, 87, 88, 97, back
cover; Russell Maynor: pp. 3, 33, 72, 79, 91; Gay Men's Health Crisis,
Inc./Peter Schaaf: p. 64.
Ken is a registered trademark of Mattel, Inc.

*Please note: All photos in this book are for entertainment purposes only.*
*The appearance of any model in no way represents or implies his or her sexual orientation.*

Published by Contemporary Books
An imprint of NTC/Contemporary Publishing Company
Two Prudential Plaza, Chicago, Illinois 60601-6790
Manufactured in the United States of America
International Standard Book Number: 0-8092-3320-7

10    9    8    7    6    5    4    3

*For Miriam,*
*the mother everyone wishes he had.*


*For John,*
*who filled this book with love.*

# YOU KNOW YOU'RE ABSOLUTELY GONNA BE GAY WHEN

your third-grade teacher asks you
for decorating tips.

**YOU KNOW YOU'RE GAY WHEN**
you still get a nervous stomach thinking
about phys ed class.

**YOU KNOW YOU'RE GAY WHEN**
a big, bearded Texas two-stepper makes you
feel like Patsy Cline at the junior prom.

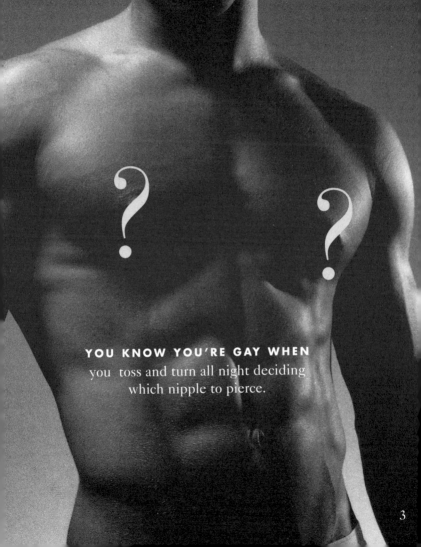

**YOU KNOW YOU'RE GAY WHEN**

you  toss and turn all night deciding
which nipple to pierce.

## YOU KNOW YOU'RE GAY WHEN...

your coffee table has more
candles than Saint Patrick's.

Jehovah's Witnesses knock on
everybody's door but yours.

San Pellegrino is as close as
you'll ever get to holy water.

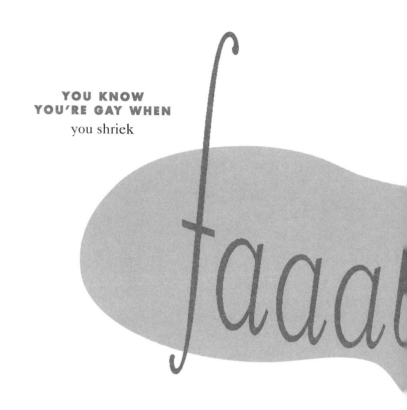

**YOU KNOW
YOU'RE GAY WHEN**
you shriek

*ulousss*!

for the very first time.

# YOU KNOW YOU'RE
# REALLY

you remember the exact date Maria Callas
made her Metropolitan Opera debut.

you spend hours in flea markets searching for
*absolutely divine* sorbet spoons.

you get these uncontrollable urges
to sing "I Feel Pretty."

# GAY WHEN...

you think a wide receiver is
a chubby "bottom."

**YOU KNOW YOU'RE GAY WHEN**
you can rattle off all of Liz Taylor's
husbands quicker than she can.

**YOU KNOW YOU'RE GAY WHEN**
you're still traumatized by
Bambi's mother's death.

**YOU KNOW YOU'RE GAY WHEN**
you've memorized
every one of *International Male*'s
underwear styles by heart.

**YOU KNOW YOU'RE GAY WHEN**
you can spot a "club" member
clear across the room.

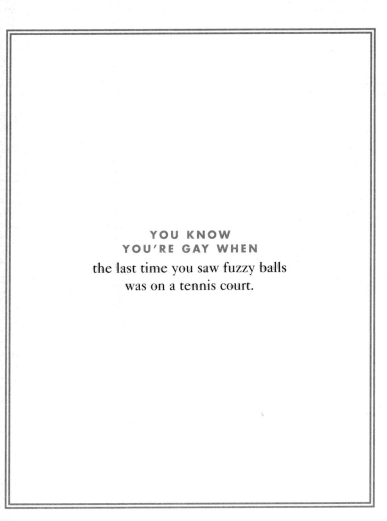

**YOU KNOW
YOU'RE GAY WHEN**

the last time you saw fuzzy balls
was on a tennis court.

**YOU KNOW YOU'RE GAY WHEN**
a fella finally holds you in his arms.

**YOU KNOW YOU'RE GAY WHEN**
you discover the pain and pleasure of beard burn.

**YOU KNOW YOU'RE GAY WHEN**
he sends you two dozen tulips and a poem—
*in French*—the next day.

**YOU KNOW YOU'RE GAY WHEN**

*you can't wait to do it all over again.*

*You know you're gay when*

you get your first teddy bear
from a boyfriend.

# BEST TIMI

### TO BE GAY WHEN...

a president finally mentions the "G" word in
an inaugural address.

the *Queen Elizabeth II* sets sail
with a boatload of queens.

safe sex sets a new standard
for love...and life.

men's underwear ads are *everywhere!*

every leading actor in Hollywood
can't wait to play a homosexual.

**YOU KNOW YOU'RE GAY WHEN**
you've got a corner office and a company car
but you still can't put your boyfriend's
picture on your desk.

**YOU KNOW YOU'RE GAY WHEN**
straight couples can smooch all night in a
restaurant but you've got to settle for an
under-the-table tickle.

**YOU KNOW YOU'RE GAY WHEN**

you realize life ain't always fair.

*Love*

- [✓] Anything from Dolce & Gabbana

- [✓] Risotto

- [✓] Clinique Turnaround Cream

- [✓] Camp

- [✓] Hairy chests

- [✓] Every Speedo second of the Olympic diving competitions

- [✓] Pillow shams and neck rolls and quilts and throws

- [✓] Cirque du Soleil

- [✓] Exploring every inch of your boyfriend's bo

- [✓] Telling people you just returned from St. Barth's

# Hate

 Everything from the Spiegel catalog

 Brown rice

 Vaseline Intensive Care Lotion

 Camp

 Hairy backs

 Every crotch-grabbing hour
of the World Series

 Making your bed

 The circus

 Sharing his toothbrush

 Opening your American Express bill
two weeks later

you read how much it costs to
send a kid to college.

# E GAY **WHEN...**

Kraft Parkay becomes America's
official spread.

you accidentally wander into a
Sears furniture department.

you share your Graceland tour with the
Mormon Retired Teachers Association.

**YOU KNOW YOU'RE GAY WHEN**
your dog is named Tallulah.

**YOU KNOW YOU'RE GAY WHEN**
your cat is named RuPaul.

## YOU KNOW YOU'RE GAY WHEN

your goldfish are named…

Blanche

Dorothy

Rose

Sophia

# YOU KNOW YOU'RE ABSOLUTELY GONNA BE GAY WHEN...

the first thing you build with your
Erector set is a doll house.

you refuse to go to sleep without Ken.

29

**arrive at a party exactly on time.**

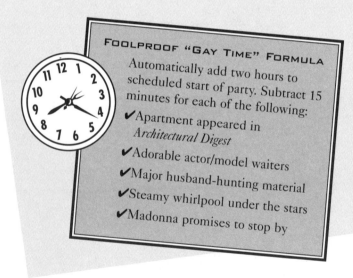

FOOLPROOF "GAY TIME" FORMULA

Automatically add two hours to scheduled start of party. Subtract 15 minutes for each of the following:

✔Apartment appeared in *Architectural Digest*

✔Adorable actor/model waiters

✔Major husband-hunting material

✔Steamy whirlpool under the stars

✔Madonna promises to stop by

# N A MILLION YEARS

parade around the locker room in
Fruit of the Loom underwear.

order a pair of Barcaloungers
in beige Herculon.

take a passport photo in anything
but a timeless outfit.

admit that your "homemade" fish pâté
is actually jarred gefilte fish.

leave a copy of *Reader's Digest* on
your coffee table.

# MOST **INCREDIBLE** DREAMS

**ABOUT...**

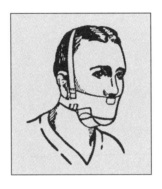

being bound and gagged in
a Sicilian sausage factory.

getting stuck in an elevator
with Brad Pitt and Ethel Merman.

everything at Ralph Lauren
reduced by 75%.

armpits, armpits, and more armpits.

**YOU KNOW YOU'RE GAY WHEN**
you take a deep breath
and sign your name next to his on a lease.

**YOU KNOW YOU'RE GAY WHEN**
your aunt asks where
the two of you are "registered."

APARTMENTS AVAILABLE—UNFURNISHI

**YOU KNOW YOU'RE GAY WHEN**
the saleslady at Macy's mattress department
reminds you that you're in a "family" store.

**YOU KNOW YOU'RE GAY WHEN**
you have your first fight over
how much drapery material
should "puddle" on the floor.

WEST HOLLYWOOD REAL ESTATE

35

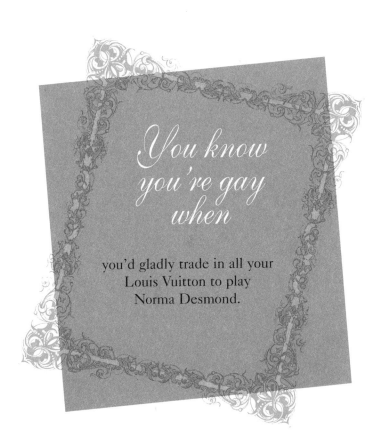

*You know
you're gay
when*

you'd gladly trade in all your
Louis Vuitton to play
Norma Desmond.

you leave a wife, two kids, a yellow Lab,
and a big house in the suburbs
for a tiny studio apartment, pangs of guilt,
lonely nights, awkward kisses, and,
at long last,
a life of honesty and love.

**YOU KNOW YOU'RE GAY WHEN**
you can saunter into any designer showroom
without being a designer.

**YOU KNOW YOU'RE GAY WHEN**
just saying *greige*, *aubergine*, and *chartreuse*
gives you a thrill.

**YOU KNOW YOU'RE GAY WHEN**
half the world has seen
your fabric swatches.

**YOU KNOW YOU'RE GAY WHEN**
you comb the fringe on
your Oriental rugs.

*You know you're gay when*
*your impeccable taste*
*becomes a pain in the ass.*

*you're gay when*

your flower bills are
higher than your grocery bills.

*You know you're*
*gay when you love*
*making love...*

with your shades opened
just enough to make your neighbor
very happy he renewed his lease.

after the sweatiest bike ride
of the summer.

tied to a four-poster bed
with four Hermès scarves.

in front of the mirror—just you,
your tan line, and Coltrane purrin'
"In a Sentimental Mood."

guys wearing construction boots
during sex.

# YOU KNOW
## YOU'RE GAY WHEN YOU'R

construction workers who sweat
in the most wonderful places.

three-way mirrors that
make you look ten pounds lighte

the word "uncut.

Venetian chandeliers in bathrooms.

# totally turned on BY...

French charm bracelets.

rubber sheets and Pratesi pillowcases.

guys from Vermont who do
the most unusual things
with Ben & Jerry's ice cream.

**YOU KNOW YOU'RE GAY WHEN**
you find out Rice Queens aren't
members of the Chinese imperial family.

**YOU KNOW YOU'RE GAY WHEN**
Castro has nothing to do with Cuba.

**YOU KNOW YOU'RE GAY WHEN**
your favorite basketball move is a rim shot.

**YOU KNOW YOU'RE GAY WHEN**
you trim your pubic hair
before you go for a checkup.

**YOU KNOW YOU'RE GAY WHEN**
you wake up one morning and discover a
man sleeping next to you ... and you have no
idea who he is.

50

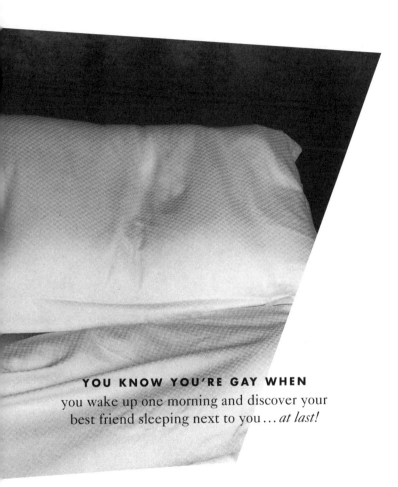

**YOU KNOW YOU'RE GAY WHEN**
you wake up one morning and discover your
best friend sleeping next to you ... *at last!*

You know
you're gay

you'd give anything to see *All About Eve*
on a bumpy plane ride.

you no longer care if the cleaning lady
finds your porno magazines.

your mom refers to your cats
as her grandchildren.

*when* . . .

Antonio Banderas makes you
drop your popcorn.

**YOU KNOW YOU'RE GAY WHEN**
you never accept the first table a maître d' offers you
(unless it's facing a mirror).

**YOU KNOW YOU'RE VERY GAY WHEN**
you send back a meal
that's too monochromatic.

**YOU KNOW YOU'RE VERY, VERY GAY WHEN**
you only go to restaurants
whose "doggy" bags are shaped like swans.

**YOU KNOW YOU'RE GAY WHEN**
you have track lighting
in your refrigerator.

**YOU KNOW YOU'RE GAY WHEN**
your Michael Feinstein CDs are
the first things you'd grab if
your house caught fire.

You know you're gay when your bathroom

**YOU KNOW YOU'RE GAY WHEN**
you've got more faux in your apartment
than Dolly Parton has on her head.

re pink flamingos than Hialeah racetrack.

# YOU KNOW YOU'R

your idea of a dream vacation is a grand tour
of every fashion outlet mall in America.

# GAY WHEN...

you hang your clothes alphabetically
by designer.

a chest that's bigger and firmer
than your sister's.

*You know you're gay wh*

a vanity plate for your Jeep that reads:

GWM-4WD

*anything* with tassels.

*u simply have to have...*

a blond personal trainer with
a hyphenated French name.

a genuine Cartier rolling ring.

yet another Russell Wright gravy boat
for your china collection.

*You know you're gay when the first thing you look for...*

in a new boyfriend is the one spot
that's absolutely off limits.

in a new office is anyone who
*doesn't* join the football pool.

in a new computer is a hunky
computer technician to help you plug it in.

in a new car is a lighted vanity mirror.

the city is ours
as far as the eye can see!

# O BE GAY WHEN...

you think about the countless hours of AIDS
volunteer work performed by our brothers
and sisters.

people like Barney Frank, k.d. lang,
Greg Louganis, Martina Navratilova, and
Melissa Etheridge kick the closet door
wide open for all of us.

you realize how dull the world would be
without the designers, artists, dancers, writers,
and performers we call our own.

**YOU KNOW YOU'RE GAY WHEN**
our political advances remind you
of a cha-cha lesson: one step ahead, one step back.

**YOU KNOW YOU'RE GAY WHEN**
Shilts, Monette, Kramer, and Sullivan
start edging out Collins, Cartland,
Steel, and Bombeck on your bookcase shelves.

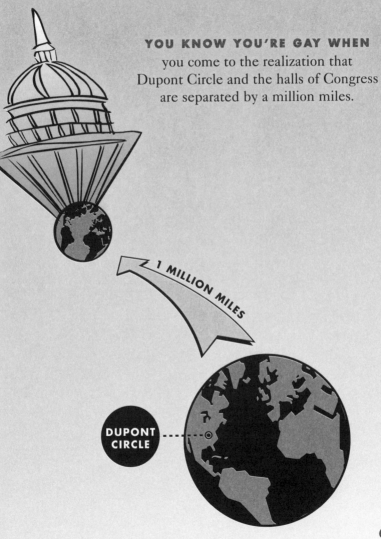

**YOU KNOW YOU'RE GAY WHEN**
you come to the realization that
Dupont Circle and the halls of Congress
are separated by a million miles.

1 MILLION MILES

DUPONT
CIRCLE

# You know you're gay when...

somebody calls you "faggot"
for the very first time.

you get arrested
at an Act Up sit-in.

SILENCE=DEATH

you proudly cast a vote for
a member of the "family."

YOU KNOW YOU'RE GAY
WHEN YOU HAVE THE MOST
HORRIBLE NIGHTMARES
ABOUT...

Newt Gingrich decorating the Oval Office
with black velvet paintings.


the Rockettes hanging up their
ermine muffs for the last time.


bumping into your father
at an S & M sex club.


the world's Lycra supply
dwindling down to two thongs
and a sportsbra.


your office colleagues chipping in
to buy you a 110-piece
Craftsman wrench set for your birthday.


Calvin Klein underwear
being bugged by the CIA.

**YOU KNOW YOU'RE GAY WHEN**
you could pee in your pants
before you undo all those damn buttons!

# You know you'r

your toiletry bag is bigger than
most travelers' carry-ons.

your flight attendant personally introduces you
to the "Mile High" club.

that adorable bellhop in Amsterdam
leaves *you* a tip!

*ay when...*

*everyone* on Savile Row wants to take
your inseam measurement.

a Parisian takes you home
to sample *his* coq au vin.

# YOU KNOW THE WHOLE IS GAY WHEN..

Hadassah offers package
vacations to Key West.

*Tom of Finland* becomes a
Disney animated movie.

JCPenney opens a branch on
Christopher Street.

# WORLD

Hot Cross Buns

Honey Buns

Raisin Buns

Big Buns

Chewy Buns

Sticky Buns

Cinnamon Buns

GOOD HOUSEKEEPING PUBLISHES
GAY PRIDE DAY RECIPES.

77

**YOU KNOW YOU'RE GAY WHEN**
you have this overwhelming desire to
blow on the neck of the train passenger
next to you.

**YOU KNOW YOU'RE GAY WHEN**
you discover highway rest areas
aren't just for resting.

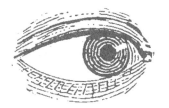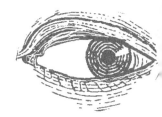

**YOU KNOW YOU'RE GAY WHEN**
the best merchandise at Bloomie's and Barneys
isn't found on the racks.

**YOU KNOW YOU'RE GAY WHEN**
a well-hung masterpiece from the Metropolitan
Museum magically ends up in your bedroom.

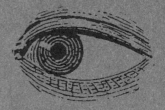

**YOU KNOW YOU'RE GAY WHEN**
you'd gladly trade three one-night stands
for one fabulous cuddle.

# YOU KNOW
# YOU'RE GAY WHEN..

## YOU CAN'T BOIL AN EGG

But you *can* whip up a
mind-boggling Grand Marnier soufflé.

## YOU CAN'T SPACKLE A WALL

But you *can* stencil an ivy border
that puts Martha Stewart to shame.

### YOU CAN'T SAIL A BOAT

But you *can* lead the conga line
on an RSVP Caribbean cruise.

### YOU CAN'T PITCH A TENT

But you *can* gather the most
gorgeous bouquet of wildflowers.

### YOU CAN'T DRIVE A STICK

But you *can* drive half of Europe
crazy as you try to learn.

83

**YOU KNOW YOU'RE GAY WHEN**
you can watch *Dark Victory*, *Valley of the Dolls*,
*Auntie Mame*, *Some Like It Hot*, *What Ever
Happened to Baby Jane?*, and *The Women* without
the sound and still know every word.

**YOU KNOW YOU'RE GAY WHEN**
you can fast forward to Jeff Stryker's greatest
moments in less than 10 seconds.

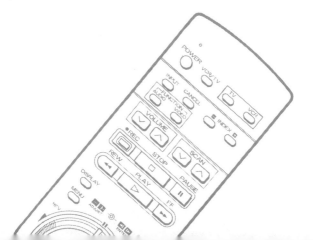

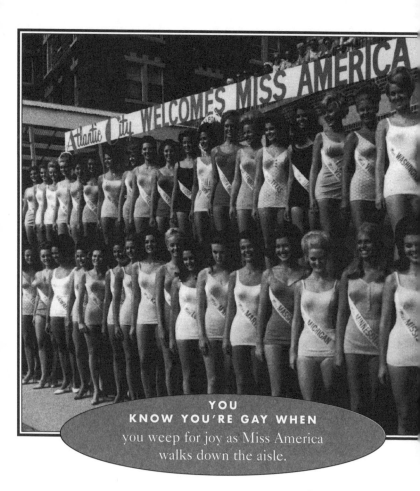

**YOU KNOW YOU'RE GAY WHEN**
you weep for joy as Miss America walks down the aisle.

**YOU KNOW YOU'RE GAY WHEN**
you've *always* got the latest dish on who's homo in Hollywood.

**YOU KNOW YOU'RE GAY WHEN**
your Lancôme representative calls to wish you a Merry Christmas.

**YOU KNOW YOU'RE GAY WHEN**
you whistle "A Weekend in the Country" every Friday, and nobody in the office catches on.

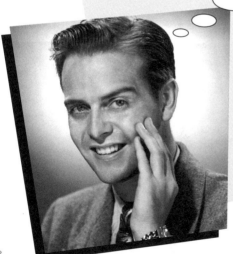

all you can think
about in study class
is playing strip
poker with your
best buddy Brad.

# You know you're absolutely gonna be gay when...

you'd give the world to have
Wally Cleaver move in next door.

the only thing you want for your
15th birthday is a Cuisinart.

**YOU KNOW YOU'RE GAY WHEN**

you dress your dog
in nothing but black.

**YOU KNOW YOU'RE GAY WHEN**
you've got a collar and leash
and you don't own a dog!

**YOU KNOW YOU'RE GAY WHEN**
*winter finds you bitchin' once again,
"I'd rather catch pneumonia
than have hat hair!"*

**YOU KNOW YOU'RE GAY WHEN**
*spring's sunny glow makes everyone in the
park look absolutely scrumptious.*

**YOU KNOW YOU'RE GAY WHEN**
*summer means kissing in the dunes
and never having a towel when
you really need one.*

**YOU KNOW YOU'RE GAY WHEN**
*fall makes you nostalgic for macaroni and
cheese from the school cafeteria,
snapping towels in the locker room, and
Mr. Hamilton, who found any excuse to
brush against you in his chemistry class.*

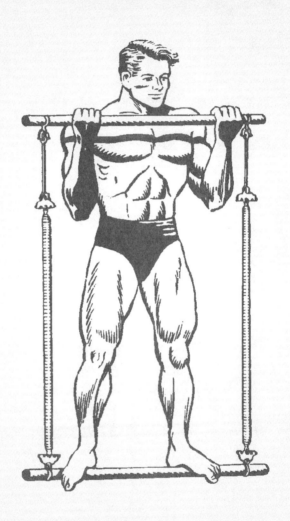

**YOU KNOW YOU'RE GAY WHEN**
you start getting mail delivered
to the gym.

# You know it's no picnic being gay when...

you're constantly getting paper cuts opening all those fund-raiser requests.

Streisand tickets require a second mortgage.

your parents still insist that you and your lover occupy separate bedrooms in their house.

discos operate on the theory that nobody has to go to work in the morning.

you fall asleep during phone sex
and receive a bill for $1,000.

**YOU KNOW YOU'RE GAY WHEN**
you're willing to hike miles from the parking lot
to be on the "Dorothy" section of the beach.

**YOU KNOW YOU'RE GAY WHEN**
you tote along enough SPF numbers
to teach a math class.

**YOU KNOW YOU'RE GAY WHEN**
summer's bestsellers can't compete
with all those tight, tanned tushes on parade.


**YOU KNOW YOU'RE GAY WHEN**
you'd love to have just one of those
tushes to call your own.

# *You know you'r*

## WHEN...

you buy a clutch purse to match your kilt.

you pick Judy or Liza as your
confirmation name.

you don't know who's playing in the
Super Bowl and you have absolutely no idea
what the Super Bowl *is*.

Tupperware nominates you as their
homemaker of the year.

BEYOND GAY

**YOU KNOW YOU'RE GAY WHEN**

you start taking figure-skating lessons
to keep Tonya's flame alive.

You know you're gay
when you've been
out of the closet for
more than half your life.

You know you're gay
when you wouldn't step
back inside for all the
money in the world.

**WE LOVE GETTING LETTERS!**

If you've gotten this far, you've probably got some fabulous
*You Know You're Gay When* moments of your own. Why not
jot down a few and send them along. Who knows, you
might just end up in our sequel! After all, one little book is
just the beginning of the one-of-a-kind experiences that
make being gay so wonderful.

**FRESH IDEAS DAILY**
**POST OFFICE BOX 1**
**NEW YORK, NY 10276-0001**

**E-MAIL: veryfresh@aol.com**